novum premium

*This book is dedicated to John Streeting,
whose benevolent spirit and unique
understanding of the human condition
made even the most displaced feel at home.*

Printed in the European Union on environmentally friendly, chlorine- and acid-free paper.

ISBN 978-3-903861-67-1
Editing: Ashleigh Brassfield, DipEdit
Cover photo:
Movement on the Ground
Cover design, layout & typesetting:
Movement on the Ground
Internal illustrations:
Movement on the Ground

www.novum-publishing.co.uk

melting pot

Breaking bread and sharing food.
Cooking with refugees
and locals in Lesvos.

novum premium

MOVEMENT
ON THE GROUND

Sophie Streeting

Editorial consultant

Movement On The Ground (MOTG) is a Dutch organisation founded in 2015 in response to the onset of the European migration crisis. Motivated to bring actionable change to the humanitarian field, Movement On The Ground's mission is to provide immediate human relief, cultivate solutions and drive sustainable change with and for people on the move and local host communities. At the core of this mission is the "Camp to CampUs" philosophy, which outlines the concept of transforming refugee hotspots into healing and dignified environments. This philosophy enables people on the move to experience a sense of community, have room to heal, nurture their skills and talents, feel empowered, generate prospects for their future and build connections with their host community.

Like the Camp to CampUs philosophy, this cookbook is a beautiful realisation that food is a powerful connector. Food can help bring forth powerful memories and, in the context of Lesvos, connect diverse people without the use of words. The stories, recipes and food of this book truly encapsulate what we at Movement On The Ground stand for: Connection, through food and through love.

Since 2015, we have all witnessed the refugee crisis unfolding on our screens, the focal point often being the island of Lesvos. The subject of this book, Melting Pot, is to showcase another side to what is usually a harrowing story. Lesvos is now home to a uniquely diverse range of cultures and cuisines. Although the dishes from both the Greek locals and newcomers to the island depicted in this book may have vastly different ingredients and styles, the common factor they all share is the warm hospitality behind each plate of food. Melting Pot celebrates these diversities, promotes inclusivity, and showcases the incredible sense of community and humanity which can be found on the island.

The inspiration behind this book came one day on Lesvos, whilst cooking with a resident who decided to share his story, the previously reserved man beaming from ear to ear. In that moment, we decided to write his story down, in order to capture his smile in the recipe he was preparing so that we could pass it on.

MOVEMENT
ON THE GROUND

We discovered that if you spoke with people about food – who taught them how to cook, what they enjoy cooking and their favourite recipes – they would immediately light up and open up. Food in the camps and on the island of Lesvos is not only a life source but a way of communicating – finding common ground, sharing, and making others feel comfortable. It's a universal language. Cuisine is a vital part of people's identity. Having the freedom to cook in the camps on Lesvos is hugely important for the residents, and they shared the dishes from their homelands with great pride. It made us realise that the comfort of cooking and sharing with others your favourite dish can give you a sense of belonging, even when you are far from what you know. As one Syrian mother told us: "It is all I have left from home."

Food has a distinctive power to unite because, no matter who we are or where we're from, we can all break bread together. Food should be used as a tool to learn, connect, and engage with each other. With this in mind, we would like people to take inspiration from the kindness, hope and resilience demonstrated by both the migrants and the local islanders of Lesvos.

Since we travelled to Lesvos to make Melting Pot, Moria camp has been destroyed in a fire, leaving the almost 13,000 residents of the camp once again without shelter. The money raised from this book is more important than ever in helping Movement On The Ground work with and for people on the move to create dignified living conditions for the new "temporary" camp on the island. From the bottom of our hearts, we want to thank everyone involved in creating Melting Pot. The overwhelming power of community, collaboration and care shown by both locals, people on the move and volunteers – which enabled us to make this book – shows us that there is hope and beauty everywhere, if you are willing to look. The book will allow the individual voices and personalities of those featured to be heard and seen, and all the money we raise will go towards Movement On The Ground's mission to enable the communities of Lesvos to thrive, together towards dignity.

MOTG

Nikoleta Makrionitou

Writer

When someone offers you a plate full of food, you should never return it empty... I arrived in Lesvos on February 20th, with a bang. I had high expectations, a thirst to get started and a certain concern for what I would find. I expected that my experience and first exposure to this refugee community would be full of spice but bittersweet. Everything I tried was life-giving, salty, and sour. At the end of each day, I was left with an aromatic aftertaste, the fiery warmth of their hospitality and the sweetness of hope. This is not an ordinary cookbook. It has filled my thoughts since the first time we met and talked to the team about the project we were hoping to embark on. The food was reason enough to capture my attention, but it's really about looking into people's lives, sharing their experiences through food, learning their stories so we can narrate them afterwards. We convey their unfolding story about the uncertain journey from their homeland to an unknown destination through strong, raw images: through their personal experiences, unfiltered and charged with world history; through the flavours that showcase their culture; through the ingredients of the present, cooked with the recipes from the past, creating the taste of their future. They generously opened their hearts to us. Hospitable Lesvians and refugees with smiling eyes, with longing, with hope, optimism, and desire to show us a piece of home. Using food to teach us their customs and habits, to explain to us their past and the influences that led to their present. This has been the most valuable experience of my life so far. This book is the dish we return to them, and it's full of wishes of good luck.

Barbara Gigilini

Writer

Since 2015, I have been following, with great interest and solidarity, the historical movement of populations from the Turkish coast to Lesvos. My emotive experience with these refugees has defined who I am today. I have met wonderful people, bonded with families, spent time with unaccompanied children who have incredible hope for the future, but also people in absolute despair. As a local of Mytilene, I have lived side by side with them in our everyday lives and worked closely to record the ever-evolving situation in the camps of Moria and Kara Tepe. I have learned from them that the value of life is what you give it, regardless of the luck that determines your course.
When I participated in this cookbook project, I saw it as a challenge. This book is a simple message: food is joy, and we all deserve the same.

melting pot

Nikos
Kokkas

Photographer

A simple idea. I always thought the best ideas are the simple ones. Asking people to cook is the easiest way of "unlocking" them. Show them trust. Give them gratitude for their effort and will; accept them. The latter should not even come into question. People from all over the world landed here, on this island in the Aegean Sea, carrying only some essentials, themselves and their beloved ones; living for today, wishing for a better tomorrow, which should not be difficult. We cooked. We enjoyed creating flavours, sharing recipes, eating all together on the floor of an ISOBOX, in a tent in Moria Camp, on normal kitchen tables, in taverns. Throughout the production of this book, we were all together, constantly. Our thoughts were pure and honest. The recipes were colourful and original. Cultures were mixed just like ingredients in a pot. It has been a pleasure... The main substance of this book is the joy of life; the salt and pepper of every wish, of every forthcoming plan for a better life. The pandemic has shown us, or at least, tried to show us, that we are all potential fugitives in our own lives. Let's not forget that.

Thanasis
Georgiou

Creative director

Sharing life, sharing food, with friends is a common practice in Greece. Sharing food in Lesvos during these days was different. Sometimes there was a melancholic ambiance, sometimes we had loud music playing and other days passed full of laughter. I spent several days with the whole team, preparing food, cooking, shooting photos and eating. Cooking always started with little words, a cautious glimpse, except when there were kids; their excitement created the right mood from the beginning. Celebration. When it was time to set this unusual table, everything changed.
Smells filled the ISOBOX's air, food was on the table to share, and mouths started to open to taste and talk, exchanging stories from back home, adventures from a difficult route which led these people to the Lesvos coast; a feeling of uncertainty for the future, with a strange pinch of optimism. And joy; the joy of the moment, the joy of people hosting us as friends in their new "home," the joy of preparing delicious food from their homeland to share with us; The joy of having a normal day at home, so rare for them nowadays and so much appreciated. Sharing food on the same table with these new friends for me, a grandson of refugees from Asia Minor, was like a Sunday lunch from my childhood...

melting pot

Stoves and bakeries

"Voras" Arnissa
Premium quality fruit!
"Voras" Arnissa

MCML

melting pot

Stoves and bakeries

melting pot

Stoves and bakeries

melting pot

Cooking with friends

This family from Syria does not have much to say, not because they don't remember, but because they don't want to remember.

Youssif & Emel
SYRIA

the story

Youssif has difficulty in sharing the details of this journey. They were forced to leave Aleppo with their children, travelling to Turkey, where they stayed for seven months. Eventually they found a smuggler that would give them a "visa" to Europe. In the beginning, he is reticent and sceptical, as to be expected. He has been watching us for a while as he prepares the outdoor fire where he will fry the kubba. Confidence comes later, as, together with the smiling Emel and their children, they create a small party. They have invited friends and neighbours, each person having their own part to play in the preparations. They even want to fry fish for us as a welcome gesture and symbol of hospitality. The table is set with a black plastic trash bag for a tablecloth and a large colourful salad ready and waiting. We all say "Shukran,"* as we sit down to enjoy our meal. Their young son translates for us in fluent English and tells us that his family is really happy to have the chance to show us something from their country. This dish was particularly special for them, mainly because it was made with real nostalgia for home and in the spirit sharing. They have been living in Kara Tepe camp for several months, where families and vulnerable groups of refugees are housed. They have made a small home in the container given to them on the central "street" of the camp. It is compact and simple but impeccably tidy. Everything from the way the blankets are folded, to the dishes stacked in the corner and the little teddy bear adorning the bed, shows a desire for structure and normality. Children are running around, while old people are discussing matters of the world and watching the chef with scrutiny. He prepares the meal slowly, with confidence and care. Emel fills the kubba and their Iraqi neighbour translates to English while the pregnant Afghan woman who lives in the adjacent container finds common ground with her own cuisine. They all laugh and share stories of their own seemingly absurd reality. Youssif wants to rent a house in the city and get a job. He is a cook by trade, and he knows how to do it well! After such a long time waiting for their lives to continue, they have no preference for their final destination, "Wherever, as long as we are safe."

01

* *"Shukran" means "Thank you."*

Youssif & Emel / Syria

Kubba is another name for kibbeh, kobeiba and içli köfte. This showstopping Levantine meatball, despite the effort that goes into its creation, is a favourite in Emel and Youssif's family. During the preparation, every member of the family has their own role. Whether served as a starter or a main dish, it gets the taste buds going.

Kubba

Bulgur croquettes stuffed with lamb

Serves 12

Dough

2 kg fine bulgur (dried, cracked wheat)

1 tsp. allspice

1 tbsp. cumin powder

1 large onion cut into thick slices

4 large Arabic flat breads torn into pieces

Salt

Filling

1 ½ kg lamb mince

3 onions, finely chopped

300 g walnut, roughly copped

1 tbsp. hot paprika powder

½ cup pomegranate molasses

½ cup oil and as needed to fry the kubba

the recipe

01

To prepare the dough, soak the bulgur in a medium sized bowl of cold water for 30 minutes. Remove and drain. Place into a food processor and combine with allspice, cumin, one large onion, salt, and Arabic flat breads, adding water until a dough-like consistency is achieved.

In a frying pan, sauté the chopped onions and mince in hot olive oil. Brown the ingredients for around 30 minutes until all of the liquid has evaporated. Add the paprika, then stir in the pomegranate molasses and walnuts. Remove from heat and allow it to cool for 10 minutes.

Take an egg-sized amount of the bulgur mixture and form into a ball. With your finger, poke a hole in the ball, making space for the filling. Insert the filling and then pinch the top to seal. You should then have a lemon shaped ball with a point at either end.

Fry in batches in hot oil on a stovetop, or in a deep fryer until golden brown. Accompany with tabbouleh salad or a mixed salad with cucumber, tomato, lettuce, fresh onions, spearmint, parsley, hot paprika, and the juice and flesh from one lemon. Once shaped, but before frying, kubba can be stored in the freezer.

GIRLS
POWER
PEACEANDLOVE
GP

"My mother taught us how to cook when we were kids," says Radja. "She left for work and the food had to be ready when she returned home. Cooking is the only thing that will make you survive anywhere, she used to say."

Radja & Hamza
RUMONGE - BURUNDI

the story 02

They grew up near the banks of Lake Tanganika in the Province of Rumonge, Burundi. Most of the time, you could find them fishing or playing hide and seek in the dense vegetation on the banks of the lake. They could never imagine that one day they would arrive at a destination like Moria camp. They have both been on the road since November 2018. They left their country with thousands of others due to problems faced with the political situation, climate change and the major economic issues that run riot through the country.
As Hamza speaks to us, we can see the longing for his hometown on his face. "We have no one waiting for us back home. I hope we can find our own new base – our new home someday." Together, after many stops from Africa, they travelled through Iran and later Turkey. They see it as a miracle that they were able to get that far without being able to communicate with anyone.

Upon arriving in Turkey, they were sent to prison as they didn't have the necessary travel documents to continue their journey.
After being released, they were forced to find work where they could in order to scrape up the fare needed to make the treacherous crossing.

"My mother taught us how to cook when we were kids," says Radja. "She left for work and the food had to be ready when she returned home. Cooking is the only thing that will make you survive anywhere, she used to say."

Both friends worked as cooks in their home country for years. While staying in the camp, the friends are both members of the refugee football team and spend their time planning their future. Radja wants to go to England to play football, while Hamza would like to cook wherever he feels safe without the threat of any prejudice around him.

ADVEN

Radja Kibondo & Hamza Muhammad / Burundi

This fantastic dish is the pride of Burundi. Mukeke and Ndagara are fish traditionally used in this East African food. They are caught in Lake Tanganyika and are extremely difficult to acquire anywhere else around the world. During their stay in Lesvos, the two friends cooked this dish with Aegean mackerel. "Fish is expensive stuff, and we cook it only when there is enough money or when we have a celebration. Sometimes we prepare it with chicken or beef instead." The fufu, on the other hand, is their famous and most common accompaniment to almost everything - meat, fish, or vegetables - and is eaten all across Africa.

Fufu with fish sauce

Fish stew from lake Tanganyika with semolina puree

Serves 15-20

Fufu

2 kg fine semolina or cassava flour

4 ½ litres water

Fish sauce

3 large, round oily fish, (we used mackerel) scaled and gutted

4 sliced onions

15 garlic cloves chopped

½ a bunch of fresh coriander without the stalks, coarsely chopped

1 green chili pepper (African bird's eye chili), coarsely chopped

1 green pepper thinly sliced

6 medium tomatoes, grated

200 g tomato paste

The juice of 1 ½ lemons

Salt

Olive oil for frying

the recipe

02

To prepare the fish, cut it in half width ways and score the skin. Heat olive oil in a pan and fry the fish on both sides until skin is crispy and golden.

In a very hot saucepan, pour a little oil and fry the onions until light brown, then add garlic, coriander and the chili pepper, and sauté for 5 minutes. After this, pop in the tomato paste and fry for another 2-3 minutes, stirring frequently. Add the fresh, grated tomatoes and cook for around 10 minutes.

Once the sauce has reduced a little, add the green peppers and let it simmer for another 10 minutes. Add the fish to the pot, then the salt and lemon juice. Cook for 15 minutes on a medium heat.

For the fufu, heat the water in a pot. Once the water is boiling, add 750g of the semolina and stir on a medium heat until you have a smooth, lump free mixture. As soon as the semolina absorbs all water, add the remainder of the semolina and season. Stir until fully incorporated. It should resemble a thick mash potato consistency.

Remove from the heat and serve it the traditional way, with the fufu and the fish sauce in two separate dishes. We ate this "Burundi style," with our hands. You can store the fish sauce in the freezer if you want to use it for another occasion.

Michopo is usually made with beef or goat, but can also be prepared with fish (when available). After frying the fish and before adding it to the sauce (see previous recipe), Radja and Hamza kept some pieces of fish aside to prepare this brilliant but simple hors d' oeuvre.
They finely chopped 3 onions and sprinkled them with salt, rubbing them between their hands to soften and draw out the moisture. They then added the juice of 1 lemon.
The fish was sandwiched between the onions in a deep food container. Ten minutes later we had a delicious, juicy, salty, onion appetizer to share.

Michopo

A quick appetizer with fried fish and onions

When the dish is ready, they give a plate of food to the next-door tent. Fekura shares the little they have without wanting anything in return.

Fekura Gabash
SYRIA

the story 03

Even if the food barely stretches round the whole family, the refugee culture is to share what they have. Fekura puts the wood on fire and cooks with reverence. There is a congregation gathered around the outdoor fire. They talk, they exchange stories, and they wait. Not just for the bubbling pot of food, but to see where life will lead them next. They fled Syria overnight as a family. When you ask them why, they say, "the war," without giving further explanation.

"Here's good," says Fekura. "We have security." Their blunt but truthful answers hide in them all the violence of a war that has wiped out a nation, none of them knowing where their journey will take them next. When the dish is ready, they give a plate of food to the tent next door. Fekura shares the little they have without wanting anything in return.

Fekura Gabash / Syria

Molokhia are the leaves of the plant corchorus olitorius, commonly known as Jew's mallow. It has been used since ancient times as a medicine for the stomach. However, when it was discovered how exquisite its bitter taste was, it was used in the preparation of a very popular Middle Eastern soup, whose rich flavour was held in such high esteem that it was named "melukia" - an alteration of the world molokhia, meaning royal. During her stay in Kara Tepe camp, Fekura prepares this hearty dish with dried molokhia found in a grocery store in Mytilene.

Molokhia

Fish stew from lake Tanganyika with semolina puree

the recipe

03

Serves 4-6

1 kg skinless chicken fillet, diced

200 g dried molokhia, soaked in water for 2 hours and well drained

2 tbsp fresh coriander, chopped

2 bulbs of garlic

1 litre chicken or vegetable stock

The juice of 2 lemons

½ cup sunflower oil

Salt

Brown the chicken in a pot with hot oil.
Add the molokhia, one bulb of roughly chopped garlic, coriander, salt, and the stock.

Simmer with the lid on for 40 minutes.
If necessary, add a little bit of water to reach a thick sauce consistency.

In a mortar, crush the second bulb of garlic and add to the pot. Cook for another 10 minutes without the lid, remove the dish from the heat and add the lemon juice.

It is traditionally served with rice.

Kostas has saved hundreds of people from the sea, mainly children and Syrians, who although having escaped from the war, they since fell into the trap of the smugglers and the sea.

Kostas Pinteris
GREECE

the story 04

The life of Kostas Pinteris, a fisherman from Skala Sykamnia, dramatically changed in 2015. Kostas came out of his peaceful microcosm to help tackle the refugee crisis by taking his small fishing boat to pull women, men, and babies from the icy Aegean waves. His boat has since become a universal symbol of life, freedom, and hope as he sacrificed his livelihood to save people in desperate need. His selflessness is an outstanding example of altruism and humanity. One that is to be greatly admired. He has memories and stories to tell that have changed him as a human being. Amongst the turmoil of everyday life with pleasant and unpleasant moments, Kostas has had to deal with the sudden "publicity" that his bravery has incurred. Neither the nomination for the Nobel Peace Prize, nor the interviews with the paparazzi have changed Kostas. He is always willing to aid every journalist, documentarist and anthropologist who wants him to share his story of becoming the big hearted "saviour of refugees" in Skala Sykamnia.

"The refugee problem is not over yet nor is it going to be unless the war is over," he explains simply, as if he has entered the story himself and knows it first-hand. "When your fellow man looks at you and without speaking you understand he is crying for help, you must help, by any means and at any cost. It is a matter of conscience; it is a matter of love."

Kostas has saved hundreds of people from the sea, mainly children and Syrians, who despite having escaped from the war, have since fallen into the trap of the smugglers and the sea. These people are alive thanks to Kostas. Even today, when he goes out with his boat, he keeps a vigilant eye; "You never know." His own port and his home remains Skala Sykamnia.
"We are not made for big stuff," he says, with a heart-breaking modesty. I look at his big hands and I think: with those hands Kostas pulled souls from the sea making safe those whose fate had been forgotten.

Kostas Pinteris / Greece

Lakerda

The emblematic lightly-salted fish of Lesvos

A generous slice of salt cured fish served with a drizzle of lemon juice, olive oil, sliced onion and olives. Kostas won our hearts and our tastebuds when he introduced us to lakerda, a simple and easily prepared appetizer, perfectly complimented by a glass of chilled ouzo. Lakerda is a savoury delicacy worth an early start to purchase the fish straight off the boats. While lakerda is a treat all year round, the locals advise that the bonito fish is most delicious from October through December. The locals instructed us; "the fresher the better."

the recipe

04

1 large bonito fish / Kosher salt / Olive oil (or vegetable oil)

Put one big bonito fish gutted in the freezer for 2 to 3 hours until it becomes firm to the touch but not frozen solid. Once firm, cut the head and tail before slicing the fish into 1.5-2 cm thick slices. Use a toothpick to withdraw any marrow from the central bone. Wash the slices, using sea water if possible.
Place kosher salt on a tray and use your hands to coat all sides of the prepared slices. Place them on a piece of newspaper and wrap the fish slices into a parcel. The newspaper will absorb all fluids and help the salt curing process.
Once wrapped, wrap the parcel in a plastic bag. Keep it in the fridge for 2 days. Unwrap the fillets, wash them with fresh tap water, and let them drain. Place into a food storage container, cover them with olive oil or vegetable oil, seal the container with its lid and place it in the fridge. You can keep it for up to 10 days in the fridge or in the freezer for 2 to 3 months.

Shukri has experienced many difficult situations including her time in Turkey before arriving on the island. "Now I'm fine," she tells us, and fills a plate with the steamy soup, giving it to us with a proud smile.

Shukri Mohamed
SOMALIA- MOGADISHU

05 the story

When Shukri's mother was the victim of an al-Shabab bombing in Mogadishu, she and her husband thought that the only safe path would be that of migration. The fond memories Shukri still holds from her home are of cooking and recipes. For her and her mother, food was their livelihood, cooking in a restaurant in the capital.
"All my life I've been cooking," she says as she cleans the vegetables with her long, elegant fingers. Her movements, though slow, show the confidence of professionalism and love for what she does. She kneads the dough for the pancakes she is serving as a dynamite breakfast.

Shukri beats it as rhythmically as if she is playing a drum. She talks, she laughs, and she's sure of the result. Shukri would like to open a restaurant, small enough to be able to care for all customers herself, along with her husband. "You don't know how lucky you are to feel safe," she tells us, trying to mask the emotion in her voice. Shukri has experienced many difficult situations including her time in Turkey before arriving on the island. "Now I'm fine," she tells us, and fills a plate with the steamy soup, giving it to us with a proud smile.

LARSSON
Orhan
Pamuk

Shukri Mohamed / Somalia

Marakh is a memorable, spicy soup from Somalia, traditionally served with the semisweet pancake called Anjero.
This dish is often prepared for breakfast, using the delicious pancakes to mop up the hearty soup. Anjero is also commonly paired with oodkac (dried meat), a favourite in East Africa.
During preparation, Shukri was glued to the stove, lovingly stirring throughout to ensure the dish was cooked perfectly and didn't catch. We were then presented with a steaming bowl of deliciously spicy, rejuvenating soup.

Marakh - Anjero

A chunky, chicken and vegetable soup, served with semisweet pancakes

the recipe

05

Serves 8-10

For the Anjero

- 1 kg flour
- 2 eggs
- 1 ½ tbsp of sugar
- 1 tbsp salt
- 7 g fresh yeast
- 1 cup lukewarm water

For the Marakh

- 1 ½ kilo boneless chicken, diced
- 6 carrots, washed but unpeeled
- 6 potatoes, washed but unpeeled
- 6 tomatoes
- 11 cloves of garlic
- 3 green peppers, sliced
- 3 spicy green chili peppers, sliced
- 4 big onions, 2 diced and 2 quartered
- 1 bunch of fresh coriander leaves, roughly chopped
- ½ cup vegetable oil
- 1 litre of chicken or vegetable stock
- Salt

To prepare the marakh, cook carrots and potatoes in boiling water until soft but a little al dente. Once soft, peel both vegetables and chop into large chunks. Blanch the tomatoes in boiling water for one minute, then plunge into cold water and peel the skin. Once peeled, cut the tomatoes in large chunks. Use a mortar and pestle to crush half the garlic and half the coriander into a rough paste. Heat the sunflower oil in a casserole pot and add the diced onion. Once browned, add the tomatoes and stock. Bring to boil then add the chicken. After 5 minutes add the peppers and quartered onions.
After another 5 minutes add the cooked potatoes and the garlic and coriander paste. Let the dish simmer for 5 minutes, then add the carrots and salt. Reduce to the desired consistency.
In the meantime, prepare the anjero. Dissolve the yeast in lukewarm water and allow it to activate for about half an hour. Put the remaining ingredients in a bowl and combine with the yeast mixture. Slowly add the water to the batter as you mix it to create an almost pourable consistency.
Knead the mixture for around 15 minutes until the dough becomes thicker and lump free. Allow the batter to prove at room temperature for 1 hour.
To cook the anjero, heat oil in a large flat pan. Put two to three tablespoonfuls of the batter in the pan and fry on one side until brown and slightly crispy. The crepes should be a tad thicker than the fine French ones. The dough can be stored in the freezer.
Serve the hot soup in a bowl with the warm anjero on the side to mop up all the spicy goodness.

The common ground that brings these two women together is that they are both activists. Life brought them together through food in Lesvos.

Mina Adali
GREECE

Sundus Avel
IRAQ

the story 06

Sundus is from Iraq, with a long career in journalism as a reporter and presenter. She managed to survive in a very difficult political situation for many years. When Sundus became a widow, she made the big decision to move to Europe with her four children. Her first stop was Istanbul, Turkey, where she stayed for several years. Sundus shows us with pride the delicious feasts she prepared back in Iraq. She is an active part of the camp's community, and along with caring for her children, she daily provides breakfast for the more than 1,000 refugees living in Kara Tepe. Sundus shows us with pride the delicious feasts she prepared back in Iraq. Mina and Sundus' dishes have spice in common, but even the names are similar due to the influx of Asia Minor refugees in both 1912 and 1922. Mina, a Lesvian local, also has refugee roots. She feels that Mytilene's evolution has always been centred around immigration, long before 2015. As a psychologist, she has a profound understanding of the trials and tribulations around people's emotional discord that has been caused by the refugee crisis. Today, with almost 25,000 refugees and migrants, Lesvos has one of the biggest camps in Europe. Thousands of people are stranded without knowing when they will leave and, most importantly, where they will go. As Mina and Sundus spend the day together, against all preconceived prejudice, they share routine such as daily shopping and cooking and embrace each other's cultures with a big smile on both of their faces. So, life continues with these small daily miracles as they both pass through the world of taste.

Sundus Avel / Iraq

Dolma is a Turkish word derived from the verb doldurmak, which means to fill, while the word sarma, used as an alternative name for this food, comes from the Turkish sarmak, which means wrap. Sundus' dolma contains a variety of vegetables. It is a matter of preference which ones you choose to use. However, the greater the variety, the richer the taste. There is remarkably little wastage from this tangy dish, with almost nothing being thrown out.

Dolma (Sarma)

Stuffed vegetables with rice and beef

Serves 8-10

- 500 g beef, very finely diced
- 2 ½ cup basmati rice
- 1 green cabbage, fluffy and not very compact, cut in half
- 3 ½ cups olive oil
- 200 g tomato paste
- 1 bunch of dill, roughly chopped
- 4 cloves of garlic, roughly chopped
- 15 long broad beans
- 3 zucchinis
- 3 green peppers
- 1 red pepper
- 6 onions
- 3 eggplants
- 2 tomatoes
- 2 tsp. turmeric
- 2 ½ tbsp citrus acid
- Salt
- Pepper

the recipe 06

Blanch the broad beans in a generous amount of water for 2 minutes. Remove the beans and add the cabbage into the boiling water. After two minutes the leaves should begin to soften. Remove from the water and separate the leaves, taking care not to rip them. To prepare the onions, remove the root at the bottom with a sharp knife. Slice them lengthways, ensuring you do not cut them in two, and beat them on a firm surface to loosen the layers. Remove the outer peel and retain the centre layers. Now move onto the zucchinis, eggplants, tomatoes, and peppers as follows: Remove the top of the vegetables to use as a lid. Scoop out the centre of the vegetables with a spoon or Parisienne scoop, so that you are left with hollow vegetable shaped containers. Chop the removed flesh of the vegetables and set aside.

Put 1 ½ cups olive oil in a frying pan and brown the diced meat. Cook on a high heat for around 10 minutes. Add the garlic, eggplant and zucchini flesh and fry for another 2 minutes. Add the chopped tomatoes and cook for a further 5 minutes. Boil the rice in plenty of salted water for 20 minutes until softened. Strain it well and mix it with the meat and vegetables. Add the dill, pepper, turmeric, tomato paste and plenty of salt. Now you have your filling. Stuff the tomatoes, peppers, eggplants, zucchinis, large onion leaves, and leaves from the cabbage (wrapping them like a small parcel).

Place the broad beans, small onion leaves that have not been stuffed and any other vegetable scraps in the bottom of a large pot. Pop the lids onto your stuffed vegetables and layer them in the pot, placing the stuffed cabbage leaves on the top. Sprinkle with citric acid and salt. Cover the vegetables with a heavy dish, slightly smaller than the rim of the pot and add boiling water until the surface of this dish is covered. Cook over medium-high heat with a lid for 40 minutes. Lower the heat and continue cooking for a further 40 minutes.

Heat 2 cups of olive oil in a frying pan until screaming hot then pour over the dolma and cook uncovered for a further ten minutes. Serve in a large baking tray or serving platter, once cool enough to tuck right in with your hands.

Mina Adali / Greece

Lesvos stuffed onions is a traditional, sophisticated dish, named after the Turkish word sogan, which means onions. Although they are very similar dishes, there are some interesting comparisons between the techniques used for the preparation of the sougania and for Sundus' dolma.

Sougania

Fine, stuffed onions with a rice and minced meat filling

Serves 5-6

350 g minced beef

3 cups Carolina white rice

6 blond onions, oval

½ cup white wine

½ cup olive oil

A large handful of chopped parsley

1 tsp cumin powder

Salt

Pepper

the recipe

06

Peel the onions and cut them lengthways until the knife reaches the middle. Put them in a pot with boiling, salted water and let them simmer for 15-20 minutes until they have softened. Transfer the onions to a strainer and run with cold water to halt the cooking process. Separate the large leaves, placing them on kitchen paper to dry.

Finely chop the central part of the onion. In a large frying pan heat the olive oil and sauté the chopped onions for 2 minutes. Add the minced meat and fry until brown.

Add the parsley, cumin, and rice, and stir for another 2 minutes. Then pour in the wine, salt and pepper, and simmer for a further 2-3 minutes.

Fill the onion leaves with 1-2 tablespoons of the mixture and place them snugly in a large pot, in one or two layers, leaving no gaps. Cover the onions with a plate to hold them down and to prevent them from unravelling as they boil. Top up with boiling water until the onions are submerged and cook over a medium heat for half an hour.

Once ready, the cooking juices should be strained and used as a jus for the dish. If the jus is too watery, reduce in a pan, then pour over the sougania to serve.

"Today was one of the most beautiful days I've ever lived here," Zahid says, visibly moved.

Mutia Alahmed & Zahid Hamoud
SYRIA

the story 07

Zahid Hamoud and his family live in ISOBOX number 72. It is their lucky number, and, for the time being, their home. Arriving from Syria on the long road away from war, which took their two sons, the grandparents now find themselves in Kara Tepe, with their two daughters and baby granddaughter. Their next path is the one to recovery which, they explain, will take some time. Their daily routine is done as a family and doesn't vary much from day to day.

This element of structure is a welcome contrast from the recent chaos their lives have been put through. Mutia cooks every day, for everyone. She prefers this to the readymade food given to them by the government.
"It's all I have left from home," she explains. Serious and quiet, Zahid plays with his granddaughter who buzzes around the box like a bee as his wife prepares us a feast.
"Today was one of the most beautiful days I've ever lived here," Zahid says, visibly moved.

Mutia Alahmed & Zahid Hamoud / Syria

A thick, vibrant chicken dish with a yogurt broth and plenty of garlic. Shakriya is what Syrian food is all about, A comfort stew-like soup, and a household staple in the lives of Mutia and Zahid.
Alternatively made with veal or lamb, you can also add chickpeas and pine nuts to jazz up this dish for a special occasion. The name of the food comes from the Arabic word "shukran," which means thank you. "Shakriya is a tribute to the good people of our lives," our hosts explain.

Shakriya

Chicken soup with yogurt and two whole bulbs of garlic

Serves 10

2 kg boneless chicken breast, cut into large bites

1 kg strained yogurt

2 bulbs of garlic, coarsely chopped

1 onion sliced

1 kg basmati rice soaked in water for 30 minutes

5 tbsp cornstarch

150 ml sunflower oil

150 ml chicken or vegetable broth

1 tbsp dried mint

1 tbsp pepper

Salt

the recipe 07

In a saucepan poach the chicken in 2 cups of water for 15 minutes. Drain the water and leave the chicken in the pot for a further 5-10 minutes until cooked through.
Add half the sunflower oil, onion, two cloves of garlic and the pepper into the pot and continue to fry for a further 5 minutes.

Combine the yogurt and 1 litre of water in a bowl then stir in the corn starch. Add the yogurt mix into the pot and rinse the bowl with 750 ml water, pouring it into the pot along with the remaining garlic, half the stock and the salt. Simmer for 10 minutes over medium heat. Add the dried mint and continue cooking, stirring until the sauce thickens.

To prepare the rice, drain it from the soaking water.
In a large pot, boil salted water, the rest of the stock and the sunflower oil together, adding the rice once the liquid is bubbling. The rice should take around 15 minutes to become perfectly cooked with a little "bite". Our welcoming hosts served their shakriya in a bowl, alongside the rice and a simple salad of cabbage, cucumber, tomato and onion, drizzled with a refreshing lemon and olive oil dressing.

The 20-year-old Mohammad explains the reason he learned to cook was to "depend on myself not other people. This you have to learn when you live alone."

Mohammad
Yemen

the story 08

Mohammad, a charming young man with a broad smile, proudly presents us with the delicacies of the homeland of Yemen. The "blended family" which makes up his tent of eight men and a four-year-old boy all get involved in the festivities, each person taking it in turns to show off their culinary specialities while looking after and playing with the youngest member of the team. The 20-year-old Mohammad explains the reason he learned to cook was to "depend on myself not other people. This you have to learn when you live alone." Despite the hardship this young man has faced, he remains positive and enthusiastic for a brighter future. "Life wants a smile," he says, and with that smile, he'll make it...

SXT JUNE

101
TO DO
WHEN YOU
SURVIVE

Mohammad / Yemen

A few years ago, the western world had no idea of what shakshuka was (an Arabic word meaning blend). But since brunch has become a popular pastime worldwide, many restaurants and hotels around the globe have included them on their breakfast menus. It is quite similar to the Greek kayana eggs (otherwise called strapatsada). Eggs are cooked in tomato sauce with spices and vegetables. According to these Yemenis, traditional shakshuka is served with zhug, a spicy pesto with green peppers, coriander, and garlic, and lapped up with malawah bread (see recipe).

Shakshuka

Eggs in spicy tomato sauce

Serves 6

8 eggs
2 large onions, sliced
6 tomatoes, diced
2 red peppers, diced
2 green hot peppers, diced
6 triangles of processed soft cheese or one cup of hard cheese such as cheddar or parmesan
3 tbsp olive oil
Salt to taste

Malawah bread

1 kg flour
2 eggs
2 tbsp sugar
2 tbsp salt
Oil, melted butter or ghee for spreading the dough and oil for frying the bread

For serving

Crumbled anthotiro or feta cheese

the recipe

08

Prepare the bread by putting all ingredients together in a bowl. Add warm water gradually, kneading continuously into a soft, pliable dough. Knead well for 10 minutes until smooth. Divide into 6 pieces, grease with oil and leave covered with a towel for half an hour.

Roll each ball into a flat disk and spread it with oil, butter, or ghee. Fold the dough into an envelope and re-roll into a thick sheet. Repeat this twice to create the flakey layers of the bread.

Fry the bread in a non-stick frying pan on both sides until golden brown.

For the shakshuka, heat the olive oil in a large pan and fry the onions, one red pepper and one green pepper. Once browned, add the tomatoes and simmer for 10-15 minutes until the sauce has thickened and reduced.

Add the beaten and salted eggs.

Cook over medium heat, stirring until the eggs are cooked. When the eggs are almost ready, add the cheese (cut into small pieces) and stir until melted. Serve the eggs garnished with raw peppers, malawah bread and crumbled feta or anthotyro cheese.

Mrs. Helen is not a woman of new trends. She faithfully follows her tradition with reverence, something she wants to leave in her legacy to her own family.

Helen Mantzourani
GREECE

the story 09

A large number of the island's inhabitants are descendants of Asia Minor refugees. Memories, stories, customs, and flavours continue to remain at the forefront of Lesvian cuisine, even today. Helen Mantzourani is one of those women. From what she knows, she is a descendant of the Greeks from Asia Minor. From a young age she has cooked, learned to embroider, and then became a housewife just as the people of Smyrni, Ayvalik, and Moshonisi traditionally did. She spent her childhood watching her grandmother, from Ayvalik, mix ingredients and create elaborate recipes, specialising in sweets and embroidered tablecloths. She listened to the way her grandmother spoke and how she behaved. Over the years, her grandmother's ways also became hers. Today, after many decades, she continues to practice the art of cooking, which she had been taught as a child, although embroidery is still close to her heart. She instils the importance of history in each dish as she faithfully plays out the "fairy-tale" of cooking. Her son Stelios and her daughter-in-law Maria Tsikna are also part of the team. Maria is another excellent cook from Sigri. She shares knowledge from her own grandmother who came from the Houchlia region of Asia Minor and adds it all to the pot. Constant quality is the trademark for this establishment.

"The foundations in cooking are the same," Stelios says. "What makes the difference is the spices in the right quantity." In the 27 years that the restaurant has been operating, the dish that remains the favourite of locals and tourists alike is "yaprakia." As mentioned before, Mrs. Helen is not a woman of new trends. She faithfully follows her tradition with reverence, something she wants to leave in her legacy to her own family.

Helen Mantzourani / Greece

Across Greece, pickles are a meze favourite for celebrating Clean Monday. Superbly simple and served with Ouzo. Greeks keep an array of pickled vegetables, such as carrots, cauliflower, cucumbers, peppers, cabbage, and celery in the cupboard at all times. Occasionally they make pickles with eggplants, zucchini, artichokes, and okra, however the most special delicacies are samphire and wild asparagus. Pickles are preserved in vinegar, and Mrs. Helen advises us that these particular jarred delights can be consumed as soon as we make them. If you have the patience to wait, their flavour becomes richer with time.

Toursi

Mixed pickles for Clean Monday

Various vegetables
(We used ½ kg carrots, 1 celery root and 1 small cauliflower)

1L water

1L vinegar

2 tbsp mustard powder

2 tbsp sweet paprika

1 tbsp salt

Clean, peel and roughly chop your vegetables

In a saucepan add 1 litre of water and 1 litre of vinegar, 2 tbsp mustard powder, 2 tbsp of sweet paprika and 1 tbsp of salt. Bring the liquid to the boil.

Carefully add the vegetables in small portions to prevent the pan boiling over.
Every batch takes around 2 to 3 minutes.

Transfer the vegetables with a slotted spoon into a sterilised jar and top up the jar with equal portions of vinegar and water

09 the recipe

Helen Mantzourani / Greece

Smelt, named marida or smarida in Greece, is a medium sized fish that is cured in a similar style to a sardine. It is a favourite appetizer among Lesvians. Perfectly paired (of course) with refreshing ouzo. The high alcohol of ouzo and its sweet, aromatic character complements the punchy spices, sharp vinegar and salty freshness of the seafood.

Cured Smelt

Awesome fish meze for ouzo

Makes 1kg

50 g coarse salt

1kg smelt

To serve:
vinegar, olive oil,
and oregano.

the recipe

09

Gut the fish and squish the heads, pressing them between two fingers. Wash them and place snugly in a salt lined food container, leaving no gaps.

Layer alternately with salt until the container is filled, ensuring that the top layer is salt.

Place a weight on them, such as a wide stone. Cover the container and leave for 3 days out of the refrigerator, at room temperature (up to 20°C).

Once they have had time to preserve, take them from the container, shake off any salt and remove the head and backbone from the fish. It should now be tender enough to come away easily.

Transfer the fish to a clean container and cover with sunflower oil, sealing the lid. To serve, sprinkle with lashings of vinegar, olive oil and oregano.

This simple delicacy can be stored in the oil for up to 3 months.

In Kabul, the affable Afghan cook maintained one of the most traditional restaurants in the area. Forzan now wants to open a restaurant in Europe.

Forozen & Negar Kheirkhaw
AFGHANISTAN - ULE

the story 10

Forzan and Negar are sisters. Along with their parents and younger brother, they fled Kabul overnight when their relatives were killed by the Taliban's violent attacks, gathering what they could, and set off on a journey which would give them a new perspective. In Kabul, the affable Afghan cook maintained one of the most traditional restaurants in the area. Forzan now wants to open a restaurant in Europe. She has a golden hand in the kitchen and superb taste that can please even the most demanding of palates. After almost a year in the camp, they no longer care about their onward destination as long as they feel safe from the system of any country that endangers them. They would like to live in a small, rented house at first, and then find a job to integrate them harmoniously into a society that will allow them to thrive.

Forozen & Negar Kheirkhaw / Afghanistan

Forozen and Negar gave us a taste of Afghanistan's national dish. A royal pilaf intended for fine dining, weddings, and celebrations such as New Year's Eve. They have cooked it countless times, yet still they prepare it with love. It is traditionally cooked with mutton and alternatively with lamb, veal, or chicken.
The art of making kabuli is an essential skill for any future bride in Afghanistan. With a shy smile they confess a candy is added to the pot to speed up the cooking process.

Kabuli (Qabili) Palau

An elaborate pilaf with succulent mutton

Serves 6-8

- 2 kg mutton or lamb, trimmed and diced
- 2 onions thickly sliced
- 2 cloves of garlic roughly sliced
- 1 kg carrots grated
- 1 cup pistachios, coarsely chopped
- 200 g almond flakes
- 200 g raisins
- 2 cups sunflower oil, (plus extra for greasing)
- 1 kg basmati rice soaked for 1 hour in water
- ½ tsp cardamom powder
- ½ tsp finely ground pepper
- 1tsp yellow curry powder
- 1 tsp cumin
- 1 tbsp sugar
- Zest of 2 lemons
- Salt to taste

the recipe 10

Brown the mutton, onion, and garlic with one cup of sunflower oil in a large pot for 5 minutes. Season the meat well, cover the pot and cook over medium heat until the meat is tender, for about 1 - 1½ hour. Add some boiling water to keep meat from drying out, if needed.
When the meat is nearly ready add the pepper and curry powder. Once tender, remove the mutton from the pan, strain and set the cooking juices aside.

Pull the meat and discard any bones.
Boil the rice in salted water for around 20 minutes and strain. With the second cup of sunflower oil, fry the grated carrots for around 10 minutes until crispy. Remove from pan and leave to drain on some paper towels. In the same oil, fry the raisins for 2 minutes, until they expand.

Now it is time to layer the dish. Grease the bottom of the pan with sunflower oil and spread half the rice at the bottom.
On top of the rice sprinkle half the meat, raisins, carrots, almonds, pistachios, sugar, cumin, cardamom, and lemon zest, a glug of the oil used for frying, and the cooking juices. Repeat a second layer and cover with a clean tea towel and a lid (if using a Dutch oven, you don't need the towel).

Cook on the stove on a low heat for 20 minutes, or if you use a Dutch oven, pop it in the oven at 180 ° C/350F for about the same time. Before serving, mix the pilaf with a spoon, incorporating all the delicious layers together.

The couple has been running a small taverna for several years, the only one in the area to entertain and feed the villagers.

Kostas & Eleftheria Hatzikonstantinou
GREECE

the story 11

Kostas and Eleftheria live in Lepetymnos, in the northern part of the island, a relatively modern village with a special microclimate created after the landslides of 1965 when the neighbouring village, Halikas, was evacuated. There, on the edge of the mountain stands a natural "terrace" above the sea, which is the nearest point to the opposite Asia Minor coast. The couple has been running a small taverna for several years, the only one in the area to entertain and feed the villagers. Eleftheria's recipes are typical of a Lesvian housewife, using local, fresh, and top-quality ingredients, cooked to perfection. Customers often make their own traditional menu with a phone call to Kostas. The couple are perfectly aligned with the quiet life of the village and have chosen to cook and care for the people who pass by. "I like to take care of the people that come," says Eleftheria. "The flavors create a relationship with people and that's what I do and I'm happy."

"Kostas is the best roaster. He knows all there is to know about good meat," she explains, smiling dotingly at her husband.

Kostas and Eleftheria Hatzikonstantinou
Greece

Barbecue Malenga

Charcoal mutton ribs

the recipe 11

Malenga is the word that the locals use for the older sheep. It has a rich and succulent texture with a warming and robust flavour. The sweet herbs of the fertile land around Mount Lepetimnos and the saltland pastures from which the sheep graze contribute to its unique taste. The sheep meat is eaten fresh, as it only needs to hang for one day.

Malenga ribs are cut thick and marinated with only salt, pepper, and a pinch of oregano. They are put on the hot grill without the use of oil, on medium heat charcoals, and grilled for 10 minutes max on each side. Some people prefer them served with a good drizzle of lemon juice, and others enjoy them just as they are. Now that's a raw and authentic taste from the heart of Lesvos.

Kostas and Eleftheria Hatzikonstantinou / Greece

This fancy recipe for stuffed lamb is like a family heirloom. Eleftheria has inherited it from her grandmother, Eleftheria Argeniotou, who was born and raised in Lepetimnos village. "I have kept the recipe unchanged. Just like my grandmother used to prepare it on her own, until the age of 90 when she finally asked for assistance in stuffing the lamb". This is the official dish of Easter, which is cooked by locals in all homes but especially in northern Lesvos. Some people also prepare it at Christmas. The scented filling has a glorious sweetness that adds depth and complexity to the dish, complementing the lamb perfectly.

Stuffed Lamb

Lesvos official Easter food

Serves 14-18

7-8 kg of lamb without the head, cut in half transversely, the upper part intact and the bottom part which includes the legs cut into portions

1 cup olive oil for baking

Filling

½ kg Carolina white rice

The offal from the lamb, including liver, heart, lungs and kidneys, chopped

1 onion chopped

1 bunch of spring onions chopped

1 tomato, grated

1 cup olive oil

¼ orange peel, finely chopped

2 bunches of fresh oregano, the leaves finely chopped

75 g blonde currants

4 lettuce leaves in thin strips

3 tbsp sugar

Salt and freshly ground pepper

the recipe 11

Put one cup of olive oil in a large, deep frying pan and fry the offal for 5 minutes. Add the spring onions and white onions, salt, and pepper, and continue to fry for a further 5 minutes.

Pour in half a litre of water, the rice, and the tomatoes, and simmer for around 5 minutes, until the rice pops. Add the remaining ingredients to the pan and mix well.

Generously season the lamb with salt and pepper, inside and out. Put the diced legs in a large oven pan.

Fill the other half of the lamb with the stuffing and sew up with twine and a large needle or fasten using toothpicks. Pop this in the pan with the diced meat and add a litre of water and the olive oil.
Pierce the skin of the lamb several times with a knife.

Bake for 3 hours in a preheated oven at 200 ° C, until the lamb is tender, and the meat is falling off the bone.

If needed, add a little water, and if the skin is becoming too brown before the dish is ready then cover with foil and continue baking.

Serve the lamb alongside the stuffing.

Mother and daughter resist modern trends, considering the traditional cuisine of Lesvos to be full of passion and history.

Irene Laskari & Kyveli Spanoudaki
GREECE

the story 12

The mezedopoleio "Hermes," in Epano Skala, is one of the oldest tavernas in Lesvos. Today, Kyveli Spanoudaki and her daughter, Irene, continue to maintain Hermes with all its golden glory, reminiscent of "the good old days". Mother and daughter resist modern trends, considering the traditional cuisine of Lesvos to be full of passion and history.

They therefore follow this tradition faithfully. This is perfectly personified in their restaurant and a delight to behold.

ΚΑΦΕΣ
ΝΑΡΓΙΛΕΣ
ΤΣΑΪ
ΤΙΛΙΟ
ΦΑΣΚΟΜΗΛΟ
ΧΑΜΟΜΗΛΟ
ΚΑΚΑΟ
ΣΟΥΜΑΔΑ
ΚΑΝΕΛΑ
ΓΛΥΚΑ ΔΙΑΦΟΡΑ
ΠΟΡΤΟΚΑΛΑΔΑ
ΛΕΜΟΝΑΔΑ
ΒΥΣΣΙΝΑΔΑ
ΛΟΥΚΟΥΜΙ
ΓΚΑΖΟΖ
ΜΠΥΡΑ ΦΙΑΛΗ
ΟΥΖΟ-ΚΟΝΙΑΚ
ΚΑΡΑΦΑΚΙ
ΤΑΒΛΙ
ΠΑΙΓΝΙΟΧΑΡΤΑ

Irene Laskari & Kyveli Spanoudaki / Greece

Soutzoukakia is one of the legendary foods brought to Lesvos and the mainland by Greek refugees from Asia Minor. This oblong, sauce smothered meatballs soon proudly joined the Greek gastronomic tradition. Kyveli Spanoudaki's version is one of the most delicious we have ever tried.
Her recipe was passed down from her grandmother, originally from Cesme Smyrna (Izmir), who came to Greece in 1922 during the Asia Minor Catastrophe.

Soutzoukakia Smyrneika

The legendary Smyrna meatballs

the recipe

12

Serves 6-8

Soutzoukakia

1 kg reduced fat beef mince
2 cups breadcrumbs soaked in water and well squeezed
1 egg / 1 tsp cumin powder
1 tsp powdered allspice
2 cloves of garlic, crushed
2 tsp olive oil
Salt and pepper
1 cup aromatic wine such as Greek Moscato (Muscat), for use while shaping the soutzoukakia
Olive oil for frying
Flour for powdering the soutzoukakia

Sauce

½ kg tomatoes chopped or grated
2 tbsp tomato paste
1 tbsp sugar / 1 bay leaf
Salt and pepper

Combine all the ingredients for the soutzoukakia (except for the wine) in a deep bowl and knead for about 10 minutes.

Pour the wine into a bowl, wet your hands with it, and shape the soutzoukakia into oblong balls.

Dust each meatball with flour and fry them in a large pan until light brown.

Put all the sauce ingredients into a pan to simmer for 15 minutes.

Add half a cup of olive oil and the soutzoukakia to the pan. Let dish simmer for five minutes allowing the soutzoukakia to soak up the rich tomato flavours.

Serve them with rice, french fries, or mashed potatoes.

Mamdou and his friend Ali walked hundreds of kilometres only to be stranded at sea for 5 days without food or water.

Mamdou Safaei
IRAN

the story 13

He laughs, he sings, he's sociable and he enjoys life. 35-year-old Mamdou, from Tehran, is a political refugee who fled his country to finish his PhD.
Mamdou and his friend Ali walked hundreds of kilometres only to be stranded at sea for 5 days without food or water. Even in their boat, before the forces overcame them, they sang about the freedom and security they would claim with a resounding hope that they would reach their destination.
Mamdou is now completing his PhD and is successfully blogging about his political activism.

Mamdou Safaei / Iran

Mamdou named his creation "Bademjan sose zorrat," inspired by traditional Persian aubergine recipes such as khoresh bademjan, mirza ghasemi, and kashke bademjan. He prepared this creamy and hearty dish to a soundtrack of the British band Queen, using international ingredients and a whole lot of flair.

Bademjan Sose Zorrat

Eggplants with special corn sauce

Serves 2-4

2 large eggplants, cut in 5cm slices
Oil for frying eggplant
Persian bread
Cherry tomatoes for garnishing

Corn Sauce

3 tbsp mayonnaise
6 tbsp yogurt
½ clove of garlic, chopped
2 tbsp parsley, chopped and extra for the garnishing
4 tbsp corn
2 tbsp parmesan cheese, grated
Salt to taste

Bread sauce

3 tbsp olive oil
2 tbsp lemon juice
2 tbsp parmesan cheese, grated
2 tbsp parsley, chopped
½ tsp garlic powder
½ tbsp white pepper powder
½ tbsp rosemary
Salt

Fry the eggplants in hot oil until golden brown. Remove the slices from the pan and drain on a paper towel.

Combine all the ingredients for the corn sauce in a bowl.

Put a blob of the sauce on the bottom of the plate, placing the eggplant on top. Repeat this until you have one or more small towers of creamy eggplant. Use parsley and the cherry tomatoes to garnish the dish.

Mix the ingredients of the bread sauce, then brush each Persian bread with the mixture.
Serve this alongside the eggplant, using them to scoop up the delicious Persian creation.

Herve and 37-year-old Guillome from the Sawa found one another in the camp of Moria, connected by the same diversity that deprived them of their homeland.

Herve Tchatchou & Guillome Nguea
CAMEROON

the story 14

"Being different forced me to leave Cameroon," says 24 -year-old Herve, explaining that homosexuality is not only unacceptable in his country's system, but often puts one's life at risk. Herve and 37-year-old Guillome from the Sawa found one another in the camp of Moria, connected by the same diversity that deprived them of their homeland. Violence and attacks are not outside people's daily lives in Cameroon, so they are pleased to have found themselves in the relative sanctuary of Moria. Herve left behind his sick mother and younger brother in the Bamileke so he could seek means to provide for them. He started the trip about a year and a half ago and hasn't spoken to them since. He worked as a cook for a well off lady to support his family and at the same time did his cooking studies. He is thinking of going to France, as he knows the language and would like to develop his knowledge as a chef. Herve speaks with a heavy tone and looks at the ground. He doesn't like the conditions at the camp, but he's grateful to have found a friend to share "all this ugliness."

Guillome was a furniture maker and one of the best craftsmen in his town. When forced to leave, he didn't know what was waiting for him on the route to Turkey. For months, he sold clothes on the street so he could pull together the cost of his ticket across the sea. His friendship with Herve enticed him into the world of food.

"In Cameroon, men almost always cook, by tradition, and women hire them to do this job. I guess I was the exception," he says humorously. He believes that even if Moria Camp is his home for now, he wins every day by cooking and learning small and great secrets from his friend Herve.

M67

Herve Tchatchou & Guillome Nguea / Cameroon

Of the many glorious everyday foods, this is one of the most typical of Cameroon. It is made with ndolé, a bitter leafy vegetable. Dried shrimp (traditionally used as a way of seasoning), is a clever addition to the dish which makes this comfort food so unique. The two young Cameroonians are unbeatable cooks. The taste of the couscous ndolé prepared by them, was as close as possible to the authentic version, given the limited access they have to some of the more traditional ingredients.

Couscous Ndolé

Spicy stew with veal, bitter greens and shrimp

the recipe 14

Serves 14-16

- 2 kg beef, cut in large chunks
- 2 kg small shrimp, fresh or frozen, cleaned and peeled
- 2 kg ndolé (ndoleh or vermonia amygdalina or bitter leaf) or alternatively spinach leaves, cleaned and finely chopped - the ndolé has a very bitter taste so if you are able to find this then rub it with baking soda and water before use
- 4 cups peanuts, skinless and ground
- 5 onions chopped
- 2 bulbs of garlic, crushed
- 7 tomatoes, chopped
- 2 tbsp white pepper powder
- Salt
- Oil

Couscous

- 2 kg fine semolina
- 4 litres water

In a pot fry the 3 onions with two cups of olive oil.
Once they start to brown, add the meat. Cook with a lid on medium heat, adding a little warm water if needed, until tender (about 1 – 1½ hours).
In a saucepan fry the tomatoes until they have reduced fully, then add them into the half-cooked meat.
Boil the peanuts in plenty of water for 10 minutes. Drain and grind in a blender using some of the boiling water. After the meat is cooked and softened add the ground peanuts, half of the white pepper, a cup of olive oil, a cup of water, 1 crushed bulb of garlic, and salt. Simmer for another 10 minutes.
Pour spinach or ndolé into a pot of boiling water and blanch for 10 minutes. Strain it and squeeze it well. Add it to the pot with the meat and let it simmer for a further 10 minutes, taking care to stir. You should now be left with a thick, rich sauce.
For couscous, boil the semolina in 4 litres of water.
Cook for around 10 minutes until the mixture begins to thicken, stirring continuously. You will know the dish is ready when it resembles a mash potato consistency. Divide two large tablespoons of couscous and wrap them tightly in foil rolls. Set them aside.
Sauté two onions in a cup of olive oil. Once browned, add the shrimp. Continue cooking until all liquids evaporate, then add the second bulb of garlic, half the white pepper and the salt. Fry for a further 10 minutes.
Unfold the couscous from the foil and serve half a roll on each plate, alongside the beef and shrimp. This dish could also be served with miondo or bobolo (fermented cassava) instead of couscous. The beef and shrimp sauce can be stored in the freezer for several months.

Her broad smile wins the customers' hearts from the moment they enter the door. She is Greek hospitality personified.

Eleni Chioti
GREECE

the story 15

Eleni set up the first women's food cooperative in Greece forty years ago in her hometown of Petra, and the second in Europe. With this innovation she gradually defined the future of her restaurant as a must visit culinary destination. With the faith that people appreciate good, simple food, Eleni Chioti did not experiment. Carrying with her all the knowledge and inspiration that was given to her by her own mother and grandmother, her food puts a smile on the face of locals and tourists alike.

"I always liked good food and this was the beginning of everything. The Cooperative started operating with authentic, traditional recipes that won over the world. Those of us who participated in this effort had a purpose and love for what we did. For all of us, cooking was a form of love for our fellow man," she explains. For four decades, her recipes have remained constant, with the same ingredients and art. Her broad smile wins the customers' hearts from the moment they enter the door. She is Greek hospitality personified.

Eleni Chioti / Greece

One of the most prestigious foods listed in the Asia Minor Greek recipe journals, this is also a formal food in Cappadocia and Constantinople. Lesvians serve it at weddings and festivals, usually with mutton, lamb or goat and fine chickpeas grown in Lisbori in western Lesvos. This is a comfort food with an impeccable taste.

Chickpeas with Meat

Festive, flavoursome stew

the recipe 15

Serves 8

2 kg of mutton (or lamb or goat), diced

1 kg small chickpeas

3 large onions chopped

1 clove of garlic, coarsely chopped

2 bay leaves

1 cup olive oil

Salt and pepper

Soak the chickpeas in salty water overnight.

Drain and put them in a large pot with all the remaining ingredients and cover with water. Bring to the boil and then reduce the heat.

Simmer for about 2 hours, until the meat and chickpeas have softened, and the dish is left with a thick sauce. If the sauce is too watery, then boil with an open lid until the sauce thickens.

Eleni Chioti / Greece

Gemata Tis Pantrias are small marzipan treats, shaped like elegant flowers, offered by the bride to her mother-in-law during the engagement. Except from gemata, they are also called "prospesmata" from the Greek word prospipto which means to kneel. The "kneel" symbolizes a gesture of respect to the mother-in-law. Although considered the traditional treat of marriage*, it is also a special gift for anniversaries, celebrations, or an offering to people whom the Lesvians consider to be highly obliging. Nowadays they are disappearing as patient housewives like Mrs Eleni, who are willing to devote the time and effort needed to craft them, are hard to come by.

Gemata tis Pantrias*

Elaborate, flower shaped marzipans

Makes 50 pieces

- 4 cups almonds peeled and passed through blender, finely chopped but not powdered
- 1-2 bitter almonds finely grounded or 1 tbsp bitter almond essence
- 2 cups water
- 2 cups sugar
- 1 tbsp lemon juice
- Icing sugar for garnishing and shaping the marzipans

the recipe 15

Put the water, sugar, and lemon juice in a big saucepan. Once brought to boil, leave on a low heat to reduce to a syrup.

Add the ground almonds and the bitter almonds. Stir well on the heat, until the mixture becomes firm like a dough (if using the essence add it once the dough is removed from the heat).

Before the mixture gets cold take small pieces of the dough and shape into your desired designs. A pear is a very common choice, but for something more elaborate, try a flower. Use icing sugar to prevent the mixture sticking to your hands.

Dust with sifted icing sugar and store in a refrigerator. When covered well, they can keep for a long time.

**Gemata in Greek means full, and this is a treat full of almonds. Pantria is slang for marriage.*

“Life is memories”, Anastasia tells us, “and mine are memories full of taste...”.

Aphrodite Milopteri
GREECE

the story

16

Aphrodite Milopteri lives in the western part of the island, in Eresos. For her cooking is a way of life. Her career in hospitality, stretching back 50 years, has left its mark in gastronomic history and her famous yogurt recipe is still being requested in resorts across Greece. Aphrodite learned to cook with her mother-in-law, who was from Izmir. She observed the measurements used, the seasoning, the art, the secrets and within a few years, she surpassed her in skill. In a baptism of fire, one evening she was left in the lurch, and she successfully fed 200 people solo. Her efforts were celebrated with a raucous “hats off to the chef.” Her daughter, Anastasia, is one of Mrs. Aphrodite's three children. She grew up in the restaurant. The milestones of her life are marked with smells, with recipes and with spices. “Life is memories”, Anastasia tells us, “and mine are memories full of taste...”

Aphrodite Milopteri / Greece

The first batch of vrasmatoloukouma is prepared in September as soon as the vrasma (fig molasses) has been produced. However, it is a sweet that is made all year round and has a rich, ripe and spicy taste. This recipe was born in Eressos, famous for its many fig trees.
Some versions of it use syrup flavoured with fresh basil.

Vrasmatoloukouma

Fluffy cookies with fig molasses

Makes 40 pieces

- 2 cups olive oil
- 1 glass of vrasma (fig molasses) – alternatively use grape or pomegranate molasses
- 1 orange, juice and zest
- 1 tsp nutmeg powder
- ½ tsp soda dissolved in orange juice *(needs special attention because it foams)*
- 1 cup wheat flour
- 1 cup fine semolina
- 1 cup self-rising flour
- 700 g all-purpose flour
- 40 almonds or walnuts for decoration

Syrup

- 3 cups sugar & 2 ½ cups water
- 1 cinnamon stick
- 1 tbsp lemon juice & 1 tbsp honey
- 1 glass of vrasma (fig molasses) – alternatively use grape or pomegranate molasses

Mix all the liquid ingredients of the vrasmatoloukouma in a deep bowl, then add all the solids except for the all-purpose flour.

Knead the mixture, gradually adding the all-purpose flour as needed until you have a firm, pliable dough that does not stick to the hands.

Divide the dough into two and form them into a sausage shape. Divide the two rolls in 20 slices each and place the vrasmatoloukouma on a baking tray lined with parchment paper leaving small gaps between them. Adorn each one with an almond or a walnut and bake in a preheated oven at 170 ° C - 338 °F for about 30 minutes.

Meanwhile prepare the syrup. Boil the sugar, water, and cinnamon for 5 minutes, remove from the heat and add the fig molasses, honey, and lemon juice.

When the vrasmatoloukouma are hot from the oven, dip them in the syrup for just under a minute each to ensure they have soaked up the delicious sweet flavours. Remove from syrup with a slotted spoon and leave them to cool and become firm. Transfer them onto a serving platter once cool enough to eat.

Aphrodite Milopteri / Greece

Gyuzlemedes are Lesvos fried cheese pies. Usually made with local, exceptional feta or mizithra cheese, and flavoured with fresh mint. They are served as a meze, in the middle of the table with a host of other appetizers for the party to share. Mrs. Aphrodite showed us how to make the sweet version. Delicious, intricate, with a scrumptious sweet and salty flavor. According to custom, they are usually made during Apokries (Greece's famous carnival season).

Gyuzlemedes

Sweet pies with mizithra cheese and cinnamon

Makes 60 pieces

Filling
½ kg dried mizithra cheese, grated
1 tsp cinnamon powder
2 tbsp sugar

Filo pastry
1 cup olive oil
2 cups water
1 kg all-purpose flour
4 tsp baking powder

For baking
1 glass olive oil
1 tbsp sheep butter

Syrup
3 cups sugar
2 ½ cups water
1 cinnamon stick
1 tbsp lemon juice
1 tbsp honey

First prepare the filo pastry by combining all ingredients in a bowl, adding water little by little until you get a smooth dough that doesn't stick to the hands. You may need a little less or a little more water, depending on the consistency of the dough.
Allow the dough to rest for half an hour.
Divide it into 8 pieces and roll the pastry into rectangles, taking care not to roll too thinly.

In a bowl mix all the ingredients for the filling. Line one sheet of filo on a floured surface and spread it evenly with the filling mixture. Roll the sheet into a cylinder and cut it into slices about 4-5 cm thick. Do the same with the rest of the sheets and the stuffing. You should end up with about 60 pieces.
Place the gyuzlemedes on a baking tray lined with non-stick paper, making sure there is enough space between them. In a saucepan, heat the olive oil with the butter until the butter has melted and the mixture is hot, then drizzle the gyuzlemedes with the sauce.
Bake in preheated oven at 170 ° C/ 340 ° F for half an hour.

Prepare the syrup by boiling the sugar, water, and cinnamon for around 5 minutes. Once the sugar has dissolved, remove from the heat, and add the honey and lemon juice. Pour the hot syrup over the gyuzlemedes as soon as they are out of the oven.
Leave to cool a little before you tuck in.

"Even if I was a very good student, racism from the Afghan government wouldn't let me excel. I want to be a pilot and I will do whatever it takes. We're ready for everything."

Medineh Amiri & Faezeh Mirzaei
AFGHANISTAN

the story 17

For thirteen years, Medineh and her family stayed in the industrial city of Bushehr, Iran, as immigrants from Afghanistan. Her husband and children hoped for a more dignified future and worked hard at the industrial park to achieve this. The contamination and pollution of the area caused them to become seriously ill. It was then that they decided to seek sanctuary in Europe. "We had to try around seven times," Medineh says, counting with her fingers, trying to remember all those nights full of fear that took them back and forth until they managed to reach Lesvos.

15-year-old Faezeh, though sad to leave school and her friends behind, has big dreams. "Even if I was a very good student, racism from the Afghan government wouldn't let me excel. I want to be a pilot and I will do whatever it takes. We're ready for everything," she says.
"Our life for many years has been on a tightrope. We know how to survive the hard times and we will not be put it down..."

Medineh Amiri & Faezeh Mirzaei / Afghanistan

Khajoor means date, and these sweet treats are shaped as such. Traditionally served at New Year's, this soft, fluffy biscuit almost resembles a doughnut. Medineh told us that they also make it for the last day of Ramadan and during the custom of Qurban. They serve them in the morning or in the afternoon to accompany coffee.

Khajoor

The sweet treat of Ramadan

Makes 30-35 pieces

- 600 g all-purpose flour
- 4 eggs
- 300 g sugar
- 1 tbsp baking powder
- 1 tsp bicarbonate of soda
- 1 tsp dried yeast, dissolved in 1 cup of lukewarm milk
- ½ cup sunflower oil and more for frying
- Crushed pistachios for garnishing

the recipe 17

In a bowl mix all the ingredients and start to knead, adding the flour little by little. You may not need all the flour to make a soft, supple dough which should not stick to the hands.

Once kneaded, cover the dough with a towel and leave for half an hour to an hour to rise and double in size.

Take small pieces of the dough and mould into walnut-sized balls, rolling them on a colander or a sieve to create a wrinkle-like design and date shape.

Put the sunflower oil in a deep frying-pan or a fryer and fry the khajoor in the hot oil until light brown. Remove with a slotted spoon and sprinkle with crushed pistachios if desired.

Pastry for Panagiotis is the chemistry of the kitchen and the art of cooking.

Panagiotis Charalabis
GREECE

the story 18

Since 1981 the Charalabis family has laid its legacy in the timelessness of the sweets they lovingly produce. It is no wonder that the pastry shop is famous for its millefeuille, doughnuts and ice cream, with the jewel in its crown being their traditional baklava. It has an unfailingly distinguished presence atop the culinary hierarchy of the island.

Pastry for Panagiotis is the chemistry of the kitchen and the art of cooking.

ΜΥΛΟΙ

Panagiotis Charalabis / Greece

Baklavou is the official wedding dessert in Lesvos. Traditionally, the bride sends it to the groom's family. It is offered as a gift as a sign of respect. According to local tradition, this gift can include either a big, quality dish or a box with 2-3 kg of baklavou. Baklavou is one of many Baklava variants, but this splendid example has status. It is tall spectacle, consisting of almost 35 layers of filo, overflowing with grated almonds. Panagiotis advised us to weight the bottom of the baklavou with more almonds so that the dessert stands on solid foundations.

Baklavou

The towering baklava of marriage

the recipe 18

Makes 32 big portions or 64 small pieces

750 g filo sheets
2 kg white almonds grated
4 bitter almonds grated
400 g sheep or goat butter, melted

Syrup
500 g sugar
250 ml water
1 tbsp glucose syrup
½ lemon, the juice

To prepare the Baklavou, grease a large baking tray with butter.

Mix the almonds with the bitter almonds.

Line the baking dish with a sheet of filo, brush generously with melted butter, then layer with the grated almonds. Cover with the next sheet of filo and repeat the process until you have used up all the ingredients.

Butter the final sheet that covers the baklavou and divide the dessert into portions with a sharp knife.

Bake in a preheated oven at 160°C/320°F for around 1 ½ hours until the surface has browned.

Meanwhile, prepare the syrup. Put the sugar and water in a saucepan. When it reaches boiling point reduce the heat and simmer for 5 minutes. Add the glucose and lemon juice and simmer for a further 5 minutes. If the syrup looks too thick you can dilute it with ½ cup boiling water.

Pour the hot syrup over the baklavou as soon as it comes out of the oven. Allow the baklavou to absorb the syrup and cool before cutting.

Along with his wife and children, they began to recreate the recipes of their father that were so loved by all his customers.

Vassilis Viglatzis
GREECE

the story 19

"Papel" in Agiasos is one of the most famous hangouts in Lesvos. The name was inspired by the nickname of Michalis Viglatzis, father of Vassilis. Wood carving was his main occupation, and he was considered one of the best in the village. This was a tall order considering the village's reputation for fine ceramics and carpentry. Along with his wife and children, they began to recreate the recipes of their father that were so loved by all his customers. Today, it is one of the most sought-after haunts for those who know and appreciate the authentic flavours of Lesvos. Vassilis loves his community and creating personal relationships with each customer. He appreciates the concept of tradition "that can keep alive the memories of time and the people who made you who you are today."

ΟΥΖΟ

Vassilis Viglatzis / Greece

Hahles is the traditional way of shaping trahanas (a kind of small sized pasta) in Lesvos, and it is an exclusively local product that you will not find anywhere else in Greece. Hahles are prepared during summer in the hot weather, so that they get to dry well under the strong sun. Like most people who still make them in Lesvos, Vassilis dries them in the traditional way. However, it is possible to dehydrate them in the oven at low temperature for several hours. Stuffed with feta cheese and tomato, they are becoming an unrivalled appetizer, but they can also be cooked into soup, the same way as pasta.

Stuffed Hahles

Trahana nests filled with feta cheese and tomato

the recipe 19

Makes 20-30 pieces

Hahles

1.2 kg strained yogurt

250 g coarse bulgur wheat

Filling

Feta cheese roughly grated

4 tomatoes, grated

Oregano dried or fresh

Prepare the hahles by boiling the yogurt for 1 hour on low heat, stirring regularly until you have a thick cream.

Remove from the heat and pour in the bulgur.
Stir constantly until the bulgur absorbs all the yogurt and becomes a dough.

When the dough is cool and firm, take a small handful of the mixture and shape in a basket. Place them in a large baking tray and cover with a tulle fabric. Leave them under the sun to dry, turning them upside down until they harden and dehydrate. This will take about 4 days. If the weather is not warm you can bake them on a low heat in the oven. Once the hahles are ready you can keep them in a jar in your kitchen cupboard.

To prepare the appetizer, fill hahles with feta cheese and grated tomato, sprinkle with oregano and bake at 200 ° C/400°F until cheese is melted. Serve them hot from the oven.

Perla

Vassilis Viglatzis / Greece

The scrumptious appetizer with the strange name, which is a local delicacy in the Agiassos area, is synonymous with greenballs, a kind of croquettes made with greens. These ones are made using koutsnades, which are the wild poppy's leaves in the local dialect. Because it is not easy to find koutsnades, we can replace them with other greens of our choice. Here we will be talking about simple greenballs, equally delicious as the type and variety of greens. The vegan version does not include eggs, but a little more potato or flour, so that the mixture holds its form.

Koutsnadoptara

Springtime greenballs

the recipe

19

Serves 4

4 ½ kg wild greens, cleaned and washed, wilted and drained
2 eggs
6 potatoes, boiled and grated
1 tbsp cumin
½ tbsp salt
½ tbsp pepper

For frying

Flour for coating
Olive oil for frying
Kefalotyri cheese grated for garnishing (you could also use parmesan)

In a bowl combine all the ingredients and leave them in the refrigerator for half an hour.

Shape the mixture into small egg-shaped balls, flour them all over and fry them in plenty of hot olive oil (if the mixture is too loose to shape them, add some breadcrumbs or panko). Once browned, remove them with a slotted spoon and place on an absorbent paper to drain the oil. Serve them hot and sprinkle with kefalotyri cheese if desired.

As a footballer playing for major Congolese teams like DCMP, life as a child was all about football. Later, his passion became food, cooking in three-star hotels.

Ronchellen & Fabrice
CONGO

the story 20

"When you don't feel safe in your country, you leave," says Ronchellen, who speaks outside the tent that has become his home, along with 11 other adults.
As a footballer playing for major Congolese teams like DCMP, life as a child was all about football. Later, his passion became food, cooking in three-star hotels. For many African countries, football is perhaps one of the only ways to escape the economic hardship that engulfs the country. Many young people use sport to gain a path to a better life. When Ronchellen lost his coach, he was plunged into mourning and made the decision that Congo was no longer for him. Holding tight onto the crucial lessons his coach had taught him on his path to adulthood, he decided to embark on his journey to Europe, via Turkey. There he stayed for a few months, finally managing to reach the shores of Lesvos hidden in a small boat. Today he lives in the harsh conditions of Moria, where he met his co-national and best friend, Fabrice. Fabrice (who is also from Kinshasa) left behind his large family. In an unfamiliar place, his love for football is what connected him to Ronchellen, and they share a common dream of playing for a great team. The two young men cook and listen to Congolese music every day. They are enthusiastic and have power and conviction that anything can be accomplished as long as you want it enough.

Ronchellen & Fabrice / Congo

Fabrice prepared us the perfect taste of Congo. Also referred to as nsaka zi madesu or saka-saka madezo, this dish is one of the best cassava leaf casseroles around. It's tricky and takes time, but the delicious result is worth every second of its preparation. As the beans were boiling and the stew was bubbling, the vibrant African music from the equatorial countries gave rhythm and colour to the cooking experience.

Pondu Ya Madesu

Rich Congolese bean stew with cassava leaves

Serves 24

- 2 kg crab eye beans
- 1 kg pondu (cassava, yucca or manioca leaves) frozen
- 2 cloves garlic, chopped
- 1 chopped onion and 4 onions cut into rings
- 2 large green peppers, cut into rings
- 1 litre sunflower oil (traditionally in Congo they use palm oil)
- 3 fillets of salted cod
- (makayabu), soaked in water and rinse several times until the salt is removed and cut into in portion sized bites
- 2 kg basmati rice
- 4 cups chicken or vegetable stock
- 2 tbsp all-purpose seasoning
- Salt

the recipe 20

Boil the beans in a big pot with plenty of water, for 20 minutes. Strain the water from the beans and add fresh, boiling water, the pondu, garlic, chopped onion and salt, then continue boiling the beans for 30 minutes until softened.

Heat the 1 litre of sunflower oil in a pan and on a high heat, fry the rings of 3 onions and the peppers. Once browned, transfer all the contents of the pan along with the oil into the pot with the cooked beans. Add the stock and the all-purpose seasoning. Continue to simmer for another half hour with the lid open, until the sauce reduces.

In the meantime, fry the cod fillets in a pan with plenty of sunflower oil until golden brown. Remove them with a slotted spoon.

Fill a separate pan with the sunflower oil, the rings from the remaining onion, then add the rice. Stir on high heat for 5 minutes.

Cover the rice with boiling water and season. Simmer the rice for around 15 minutes, until softened.

Serve the pondu ya madesu with the fish and rice. The bean stew can be stored in the freezer.

His shop menu is an homage to his mother's favourite recipes and brings forth beautiful memories of the life he left back in Damascus.

Mehmoud
SYRIA

the story 21

Mehmoud is one of the first refugees to open a food shop in the city of Mytilene. He only shops from local suppliers and has managed, in a short time, to gain a wide range of clientele and the trust of the locals in the market. Serious and concise, he speaks directly about the difficult course of his life. He was uprooted from Damascus and, after walking thousands of miles, reached the shores of Lesvos in a plastic boat.
He has spent four years living in Lesvos, taking a few breaks in other parts of Greece where he volunteered, providing meals for refugees. Although his initial preference was to live in France, he now says he prefers Greece. He feels that the people here are closer to his own culture and, among other things, the Syrians who remain on the island are now also part of his community.

Mehmoud is a doctor, but he now knows his goal is to survive. What he can do just as well for people's "well-being" is to give them the flavours of his country. His shop menu is an homage to his mother's favourite recipes and brings forth beautiful memories of the life he left back in Damascus. He really likes the island of Lesvos and hopes, in the future, to continue working as a doctor. He is happy that he managed to embed himself in the country's economy by being a shop keeper and he is proud that he contributes, just as the Greeks do. Mehmoud believes that through the crisis, opportunities are born, and presents himself as a living example of how to take them. It is his belief that every refugee is an ambassador of his country, but at the same time he understands the defensive attitude that some locals hold against them. Mehmoud is a shining example that with the right conviction, everything is possible.

Mehmoud / Syria

There are countless variations of baba ghannouj from Middle Eastern countries. They differ mainly in the selection of spices, but most of them contain tahini. This vibrant eggplant salad is healthy, gluten free, and vegan. Mehmoud makes a very refreshing and light version. We had the pleasure of sampling it with baked Arabic bread.

Baba Ghannouj

A glorious Syrian eggplant salad

the recipe 21

Serves 8

5 eggplants, baked in the oven grill or even better on the charcoals

1 firm tomato

½ white onion

2 green peppers

1 red pepper

1 bunch of parsley, without the thick stalks

1 small clove of garlic

2 tbsp pomegranate molasses

2 tbsp olive oil

A squeeze of lemon

Salt

200g walnuts roughly chopped for garnishing

Roast the eggplant and the peppers on hot charcoals or a grill, then leave to cool. Chop all the vegetables, season with salt and mix in a deep bowl. Serve with a garnish of walnuts, olive oil, a squeeze of lemon and pomegranate juice.

Mehmoud / Syria

Shawarma is the epitome of Levantine street food, a real crowd-pleaser. Made in the same style as the Greek souvlaki, it is very popular in many Middle Eastern street food eateries. Syrians traditionally use lamb or mutton and, more recently, chicken, beef, or turkey. Pieces of meat fillet are placed on a vertical spit and roasted on a rotisserie, in the same way as gyros (shawarma means rotation in Arabic). As the spit rotates the meat is shaved into very thin slices and served in Arabic wraps along with some other traditional accompaniments.

Shawarma Sandwiches

The definition of Levantine street food

the recipe 21

Serves 7

1 kg chicken, fillet without skin and bones, cut into small pieces
1 tbsp coarse salt
1 cup vinegar

Marinade

½ lemon, pips removed
½ orange, pips removed
2 tbsp yogurt
½ cup white vinegar
½ cup oil
½ tsp pepper
½ tsp 7spices mix
¼ tsp ginger powder
1 tbsp anise powder
1 tbsp nutmeg powder
1 tsp saffron
½ tsp cardamon powder
1 cup water / Salt

Sandwiches

7 Arabic pita breads
2 onions in thin slices
1 bunch of parsley, without stalks, coarsely chopped
2 potatoes
Pomegranate molasses

Put the chicken pieces in a bowl and marinate with vinegar and salt for half an hour. If they are not covered by vinegar, top up with water so that the chicken is immersed in the liquid.

Combine all the marinade ingredients, the orange and lemon along with their peel, and blend into a pulp.
Drain the chicken and cover with the marinade.
Soak for about 2 hours.

Bake the chicken along with its marinade in a greased baking pan in the oven at 200 ° C / 400°F for about 40 minutes till the meat is brown.
Remove and cut into very thin slices using a sharp knife.

Meanwhile prepare the potatoes by parboiling them in salted water for 10 minutes. Thereafter slice them and fry in hot oil.

Prepare the wraps by filling the pita breads as per preference.
Wrap up tight and serve it, according to Syrian tradition, with mayonnaise and pickled cucumber.

They grew up with the motto that the foundations of everything were built from our villages, even when there was no electricity or water.

Euphoria Mouka
GREECE

the story 22

Sisters Anna, Christina, and Euphoria, together with their mother Margarita, turned their father Kostas Moukas' dream into a fairy-tale reality. As an immigrant himself in New York, he returned 30 years ago to his village, Milies, an abandoned town with just three inhabitants. This gave him status and a place in history. However, when his fate cut the thread of life, his children continued to pursue his dream with the same passion. They took the reins of an alternative tourism business in Toumba (Toumba Eco Farm) in the mountainous region of Plomari, Lesvos. They grew up with the motto that the foundations of everything were built from our villages, even when there was no electricity or water.

Cooking became a way of communicating for them, a way of meeting those around. This enabled them to exchange knowledge and ideas with the villagers, making everyone's everyday life more meaningful. Today, food, for these three sisters, continues to be a code that brings people closer together. When they don't cook, they travel, learning the most unlikely cultures and adopting anything that can enrich them further.

Euphoria Mouka / Greece

This is one of the many delicious ladera (a category of vegetable dishes cooked in olive oil) that Greek gastronomy has to offer. It is made mainly in the winter months when the leeks are sweeter and especially during the fasting period. In Greece, it is argued that ladera dishes taste even better the day after preparation and can be enjoyed either lukewarm or cold. They are often accompanied with rustic sourdough bread to mop up the comforting goodness of the premium Lesvian extra virgin olive oil. If not in a fasting period, feta cheese is a must have addition.

Leeks & Carrots

Vegan delight with winter vegetables

the recipe 22

Serves 4

10 leeks
2 carrots
2 onions
1 garlic clove
2 tbsp tomato paste
5-6 sprigs of celery
The juice of 1 orange
1 tsp turmeric
2 cups olive oil
Salt and pepper to taste

Chop the leeks, carrots, and onions into large chunks. Finely chop the garlic and place them all snugly into a baking tray. Add the remaining ingredients and 1 cup of water.

Bake in a preheated oven at 180 ° C / 350°F for about 1 - 1½ hours. If necessary, add some warm water so the dish does not dry out.
Once ready, you should be left with a deliciously thick winter stew.

melting pot

Friends and Families

ELCO

melting pot

Friends and Families

Footnote

Most recipes were made to feed large groups of people. Instead of adapting these proportions to serve a smaller amount of people, we left them as they are to add to the story around how each dish was made. That's why the amounts of ingredients for each dish are so large. You can of course divide them so that they correspond to fewer people. In this case you should take care to adapt the cooking times if required.
For some recipes, where specified, there is also the possibility to keep a portion in the freezer. Most ingredients used in the dishes can be found in your local supermarket, however, some may be a little harder to find and can be sourced in stores specializing in the respective cuisine.
Most of the recipes are traditional foods. Although some are not hugely elaborate, the personality of the cook, the heritage and the uniqueness formed by their family environment, makes them special.
It is possible that they are not exact copies of the classic recipes recorded in their national cookbooks. But these small peculiarities give colour to the dishes and offer an incomparable taste, expressed by the love and skill of each cook.

Melting Pot

Editorial consultant
Sophie Streeting

Contributing writers
Nikoleta Makrionitou
Barbara Gigilini

Photographer
Nikos Kokkas

Design and layout
Thanasis Georgiou

Property of
Movement on the Ground
Aambeeldstraat 34
1021 KB Amsterdam
www.movementontheground.com
info@movementontheground.com

credits

Acknowledgements

A huge thank you to everyone involved in making this book happen. There are too many to name, but we could not have done it without you.
Thank you to every local Lesvian and resident of the camps who donated their time and passion to cook for us and share their beautiful recipes.
Thank you to the coordinators at Movement on the Ground: Rosa, Anne, Chloe, Saskia, Ali, Anouk, and Emma, who took time out of their busy days helping others to organise this project.
Thank you to Nathalie, Eleni, Lonneke, Toni and Stephanie from the MOTG Amsterdam office who helped us promote the book, reach our fundraising targets and get it off the ground.
Kind thanks to Michalis Sifnaios who opened his home for us to prepare and shoot Shukri's dish. Huge thanks to Vivi Konstantinidou and Lefki Leontidou who edited, read and re-read our texts.
Thank you to Tawab, Siad, Beshireh, Mohammad, and Radja, who translated for us and enabled us to get these incredible recipes and stories on paper.
To Alkis, Adonis, Whirly Wines, Daphne and Chloe Vineyard, and U+I, who were a huge support in many ways.
Thank you to Richard U, Richard B, Matthew, Martyn, Mike, Jonathan, and Mark, whose overwhelming generosity enabled us to get Melting Pot out there.
Finally - thank you to everyone who donated their money to make this project happen.

The author

The stories and recipes were collected by Nikoleta Makrionitou; top food journalist and Food and Wine editor of Greece's "Gastronomos" Magazine and Barbara Gigilini. Barbara is a Lesvos based journalist and owner of popular newspaper Politika. She has followed the Migration crisis closely since 2015. The photos were captured by the talented Nikos Kokkas; an Athens based photographer and writer, whose most recent work can be found in the highly acclaimed "Locked Down" exhibition.

Sophie Streeting created this project for Movement On The Ground, whose mission is to provide immediate human relief, cultivate solutions, and drive sustainable change with and for people on the move and local host communities impacted by the European migration crisis. Sophie has a passion for cooking and humanitarian work and has previously worked in hospitality. Sophie is currently working as an Education Coordinator with MOTG working in RIC Lesvos.

novum PUBLISHER FOR NEW AUTHORS

The publisher

He who stops getting better stops being good.

This is the motto of novum publishing, and our focus is on finding new manuscripts, publishing them and offering long-term support to the authors.
Our publishing house was founded in 1997, and since then it has become THE expert for new authors and has won numerous awards.

Our editorial team will peruse each manuscript within a few weeks free of charge and without obligation.

You will find more information about
novum publishing and our books on the internet:
www.novum-publishing.co.uk